A

SEASON

OF

DECAY

W.S. PRINCE

TABLE OF CONTENTS

As the sun rose upon the city, with bells tolling somewhere in the distance, a man sat in a diner with a cup of coffee and an unopened book, enjoying the comfort of solitude. He scowled from time to time on account of the stink of his cigarette which he liked to refer to in his mind as the dog of life's enemy; a friend. His meaning making mind scrambled, trying to organize an understanding in a world where everything tended towards chaos. On the other side of the window, a species that only yesterday existed in billions - - was dying like flies.

His eyes, are drawn to a group of five girls crossing the street, disrupting the wonted ambience of the season with their gaiety. A band of men leaning against the walls of a pub (probably unwinding from the smell of crowded humans) with base passions at peak; lips loosened and their moral imperative of decency disrupted by indulgences of the previous evening. They fail to be blind to the barely clothed bodies passing by. Of course, nobody would blame the men for being drunk on a Wednesday morning, lucidity had become detrimental to sound minds and only a fool would form negative opinions towards the girls for being more skin than clothing, for it was already a thousand degrees. Despite all this, the men utter words he'd never heard before. Words, I'm afraid, I'm too young to quote.

The scapegoated girls, with their fevered bodies, watery eyes, glistening foreheads and shaky hands shut their ears to the men's voices and quickened their pace in hopes to liberate themselves from the constraints of the ridicule and possibly, the other horrors these men could impart. Clever, for in such situations their lives were as much in the men's hands as they were in theirs, especially with no one but occult beings to protect them if they had chosen to advance. They succeed, now with their have secured, they'd soon be pestered by boredom.

The man in the diner, fancies to himself that members of both groups are most likely to have inward weepings. Maybe inward gnashings of teeth when in the comfort of the shadows, or in their emptiness. Those were the routine effects of the growing fear of death, he supposed.

"Ah, who would've known...these godless gods would be put down by some, pandemic? Freed, from this perpetual headache. Freed...from living life, at the verge of bursting into tears. Maybe it's only me? Perhaps other men didn't have as much difficulty living as I had had...but who cares? Tomorrow, tomorrow we shall all just be apparitions. But then again of course, to have never been born was best, for everyone; sixteen-fold."

The man in the diner - the Bethlemite, said these words in short staggered whispers, to himself, the only salesman of alternative viewpoints he had ever bought from. He knew, in that season, nothing was going to be alright, the best they could do was to adjust. Nobody could exert their will on the circumstances. The rich and the poor had become one, brought together by the child of the season and their once unwavering hope, had now been stranded in a waterless desert. Optimism had become an act of defiance to personal will and no rule of logic could conjure up a rational way to look at things now. The brave few only managed to have their patience for bearance to limp on a while before they too were defeated...knocked out senseless, for good.

***

The eight-legged question that scurried after every man's mind in that season, was whether he would press on with braving the elements or simply admit defeat and not prolong the inevitable. This question was of course of no importance to the Bethlemite. He despised those who shook in their boots at the thought of doing what they thought was best for them.

"The second guessers, the hesitant, the cowards, puppets of the masses, accommodators to every eye in the room...those little lovers of the beaten path! Disgusting."

For him, he had long decided that life had been for the living. But of course, if he had had a choice, he would have preferred to shuffle off the mortal coil in a more "upstanding" manner.

2

"A departure in which I would feel like I was more than just a mere man. One in which those who got wind of, would be proud that my feet had strode this surface, that I had borne the name of man. They wouldn't even have the audacity to say I died. No, they would say Friedrich's boy was "spit out" by life for I would have chosen to end as a man whose only and final desire was to defeat life herself, she who feeds on desire. Even death himself would deny me. Instead, both entities would leave me suspended between themselves. Neither dead nor alive. Like a checkmated king in chess who is never captured or killed. All this until either one, is coerced to open their gates. What better way to achieve this but to deny the most basic of items that life uses to keep us sellotaped to her? To be a hunger artist, with no audience. It is only such a case where one is allowed to stare back at life, laugh and cease in triumph."

He chuckled, ashed his cigarette and took a sip of the cold brew coffee. He knew it was perhaps too late for all this nonsense. Everything had changed. At that stage of the season, there was no more time for strength and bravery. Everyone had given in to the feeling of decay. Some sort of delusion, Cotard's? No, it wasn't that however it wasn't altogether false. It was a decay of something within us, something intangible. The decomposition of some transcendental innocence they had never known to have possessed, until it waned out past some dangerous threshold. The symptoms manifested in the way people now carried themselves around. Moving as if their limps had become too heavy. The sound of their words, like the words of men reading from a teleprompter, like men trying to remember something grave that they had forgotten. Their gaze? The gaze of men who weren't looking at you but through you, behind and beyond everything else in view. Men staring at themselves.

One could almost call this decay anything and get away with it, undisputed. Even those who had previously claimed to have been ordered by divinity avoided the conversation. The Bethlemite, had failed to understand it himself. When asked to explain it, it suddenly contorted into an ineffable mystery and made him feel like he had been asked to project a stranger's dream. For these (and other) reasons he had decided that there was not going to be shame in his defeat. He would become a willing victim to all of it. There was no more point in wasting mental effort in those things. All he could do when the curious parts of his mind pelted such questions at him was to laugh in answer.

Nobody could save him. It was different now from back then when the words left on paper by the wisest of man could caress his monotonous sorrows. However today at the peak of the season, at the final dance, them not having their bodily presence at the moment felt different. Them not being here to confront the future with him and that faint persistent idea at the back of his mind that they too had succumbed to time and age, syphilis, failed lungs, Alzheimer's or whatever - to lesser tragedies, gave him no solace. They too had decayed. Yes, and his time was here, he was alone and he'd die as he'd been born. Like the title of the book that lay in front of him, he felt like it really was his turn for "A season of   *decay."*

Pathos

<u>*Happiness is a distraction*</u>

How weary I am, of this mornless gloom of sadness.
this sombre life, I bear from dawn to dawn,
nabbed by the nape, by slews of dancing demons.
but, of the spoken wrests, I will not weigh to loosen,
for I'm aware pursuits outside the compass,
of this maddening sadness, are - but a distraction.

<u>*My narcissus*</u>

I loved you yesterday
without reason,
whispered to myself
that the situation wasn't
as dire as it seemed,
that at least...
the sky wasn't falling.

in that vile weather,
like everybody else
I cobbled together
the emaciated little
lumps of love I held,
and conjured an insanity
which drowned all reason.

love-weary and wanton,
you then brought to
lament all I had gathered,
scotched all testaments
of my effort, when you
chose to kiss the brow
of the crowd,
consigned to the grave
memories I had reckoned
immortal.

and so today I am,
afraid of the fantasies
my convalescing mind
dwells on...
to watch you wither
when the crowds vanish,
unwatered and alone,

unshadowed from
the harsh unpitying sun,
shaken, back and forth
by the two-faced winds.

I'm miserable when I'm alone. I'm much more miserable when I'm in the company of those who like me, especially when I'm hinted I can't soften the blows of this tragedy [life] on them. On the other hand, I feel less burdened when I'm in the company of those who do not like me. There's no need to try to do anything for them except just to be a witness. Put simply, the company of those who love me hurts me whilst that of those who hate me disburdens me. So, it comes to reason why I dislike all those I'm acquainted with whilst I plant kisses on the foreheads of strangers on the street.

<u>*If we had never met them*</u>

If we had never met them, who would then have told
about how one day we were shocked to find ourselves alive,
-- robbed from a peaceful oblivion,
because victims before us kept foundering to their sexual
instincts?
how, we were forced to succumb to societal demands,
given time to strengthen then initiated into an adulthood
where we were asked to pay to sustain what we had not asked for
otherwise, we would be laughed at and left to starve.
how, the bare bones of society trapped us into situations
where we had to throw ourselves into strange relationships
(most with neither yesterdays nor tomorrows to parade)
to ease the tasks we had at hand whilst being slowly euthanized.
how, even though we couldn't make heads or tails
of the reason why genuine smiles were infrequent,
we stuck around and pretended to enjoy all of it,
often going out of our way to be kind only to be later betrayed.
If we had never met them, who then would have told them
what living really felt like?

*I have become a spectator to my own life,
as I watch the demons tug and pull on my
everyday affairs.
I leer as they make decisions on my behalf
while I lie there paralyzed by fear, lack of
understanding and indecisiveness.
I have long lost control of serious affairs,
bothered most by trivial ideas
and only too often I have to beg my
demons, to let me laze my eyes or devote my
reveries to a single cause.
I acknowledge my presence in this transient
frame but with the shadows that have
claimed my soul, I feel powerless.
my motions and my musings have long
ceased to cause any wrinkles in the waters of
my existence,
and thus as I persist in running out of reasons
to brave my being I feel this human
existence has become too heavy to bear and
it has been anything but beautiful.*

_Light, they call her – aglow
but still shadowed by the pain she's felt.
a skeptic – of every move but tell me,
how can she not when behind every
door she's opened only sadness has
stood?_

_she is - the bright bound between
disabling self-loathe and diffidence.
a warm heart,
embraced by feelings of inferiority
and a stifling doubt of oneself._

_perhaps; if someone saw the incubi that
shroud her, then just maybe,
her tale would be likened to the tempest
before the arc of promise towers against
the vast blue._

<u>Methuselah</u>

Methuselah, methuselah,
oh please let go of me.
free me of the constraints
of your abounding presence,
your malicious whispers,
and your other horrors.
you weren't good for me then
and neither are you now.
I've borne the abyss
and now I'm weary,
set things to rights and
let me wither before dawn
--sink into a peaceful oblivion.

<u>*Cursed with intelligence*</u>

Sometimes I wish I could box all

the bad things I've done,

bury with them the sad things I've

seen and obliviate the shaming

things I've said,

to fix the scars of the sores I've

suffered.

sometimes I wish I tended not to

remember,

so I wouldn't learn from the past

for the past confiscates my

confidence,

it consumes parts of me slowly,

enfeebles my everyday charisma

and cripples my sanity.

I wish to lead a happy life with neither

regrets nor painful flashbacks,

but because I'm cursed with

intelligence,

whenever I'm alone, scenes of my

misfortune play over and over

again so vividly in my mind.
<u>*If only one could*</u>

If only one could separate

her mind and body one would,

they would love her then and

cherish her for the sequence

impulses run through her

mind is immaculate,

and the speed - unparalleled.

but with her elegant frame

and to some extent - her eyes,

comes certain responsibilities

she mostly fails to handle

and also chances girls her age

are frowned upon for wanting

to wash their hands of.

<u>*#2*</u>

There are an infinite possible courses of action in each moment but everything that comes to my mind seems either vain or trivial. Instead I choose to assume a gaze fixed on nothing for I can't bear to look elsewhere than within me.

<u>Burdened</u>

Burdened by the recurring blows of
existence;
society, culture, morality and
illusions of togetherness and mutual
understanding
it is only today, at this moment, at
this hour that I'm able to twist up my
facial features into a genuine smile,
where I feel no need to go about the
process merely out of politeness for
at this moment, It comes naturally.
it is only today at this moment at this
hour that I perceive a horizon in the
distant of something that I've not
known for so long, of something that
I'd forgotten the taste of, a feeling that
had long escaped my bones.
it is only today, at this moment, at
this hour when her warmth and scent
are only a heartbeat away, that
maybe I can assume there's more to
life than pretence and despair.

<u>Too late</u>

The ever-disappointing sun is already
upon us.
another day of nothing, I call my
cats name,
I'm ignored, nothing new but on this day
it stings.

I stare at my stout arthropod bearers
(to places I never want to be).
I think. maybe today is the day I'll get
to do it
but, its too late he says, things have
already taken place.

Seneca says if I like I can always go
ahead,
Schopenhauer will think I failed to exert
my will,
Sartre. Sartre? He caused me pain,
I owe him no second.

It's two hours before I have to sit down
behind a desk
to learn to be able to prolong my
patient's pain,
to learn to earn to afford, cat food,
cigarettes and wine.
to be reminded again that I'm twenty-
two years too late.

#3

Why cry for me now when all I've done since unfettered thought touched my mind was wish to be excluded from any future whatsoever?

Chasing dark and xanthous bumble bee,
fellow creature -- another animated
assemblage of dust, come you falsely
alleged lowly being, I have observed you,
each morning humming hopelessly
-- bumbling from bloom to bloom.
come come, but need not be angry with me
a fellow sufferer, rest a while on this
my fragile finger and if your wish persists
you may later sting but for now, let us
not let care torment us, banish from
your thoughts the decapitated daisies
and I will pause my mourn for all
-- the miseries of man.

<u>*Pain*</u>

Take off you old scourge,
set forth for another place.
with your carnal sufferings,
and nous tribulations.
leave our hearts and souls,
in unremitting rapport.
and our mortal parts,
numb to your repercussion
without strange medicine,
flowing in our vessels.

_Why prize my lungs
when all these days
are filled with tears,
when my forlorn frame
is only permanently,
burdened by sorrow?
to the dull morrows
my fear like a shadow
always seems to follow,
and perhaps before
my soul touches thirty,
my breath on earth,
-death shall borrow._

To Nina

The feeling? I'm failing to
comprehend.
on the temples either side of my
head it pains,
under the covers of my eyelids
is an ocean waiting to be let out,
and a grumbling volcano lies
at the bottom of my heart.

not! that I hadn't suspected
another lad had picked my lucky
coin,
but it's this one picture of you
and him,
that put a match to all my
unexplainable emotions.

just a glimpse of the art made
me realize,
you've given this luck-favored
lad more
in two months,
than you've ever tried to give to
me
in four years.

why? I cannot be the one to
forget
I've tried to perceive-but still I
fail.
I guess it's all the memories of

you and I I'll,
forever fail to forget.

<u>Cast aside thoughts</u>

Sometimes. most of the time,
when I'm alone and cast aside by sleep
I long to witness blood shed
from an overly abused forearm vein
to count, drop by drop
as I watch the claret red liquid
trickle slowly - but surely,
onto my vinyl bathroom floor,
staining, the white servile tiles.

I inhale deeply, then pause simply
to let...that familiar metallic smell
fill up my nostrils,
if for no other reason, than to bolster
confidence in my current state
of being alive, imprisoned
and somewhat conscious
in a disgusting, decaying
human body.

<u>*#4*</u>

Whether I'm feasted upon by mosquitos or worms, it doesn't change anything. I feel sorry for those who think they need me around. They shouldn't for I'm nothing but an insect.

<u>*Destitute of hope*</u>

I become destitute of hope,
about everything, sadly, as I realize,
the sum of the marvelous episode,
of our past eve's adventure,
was all a flight of fancy.

the small talk we had,
the short poem we read,
the brief touches we shared,
the piece of liver we fried,
were all woefully to read,
phantoms of my mind.

what did it all mean?
was it a fleeting look at,
what could've come to being,
if I had taken a certain path?
or it was just the Benevolent Beings,
making taut my severed heart?

<u>#5</u>

Am I just a luckless hobo trekking along the bustling thoroughfares of time?

A few minutes before morning

soon to be poorer by a day.

a few days left on the calendar

before the virus sweeps us up.

a few moments then left to wander,

parts of our minds we tried to elude.

places we shied away in daylight

because we dreaded to self-resent.

those days of misplaced priorities

and rigid adherences to ideas insane;

to have sworn to never have children,

to have not journeyed to Mumbai.

those decades we watched pass by;

angry with those we claimed we loved.

chasing illusions which only vanished

like apparitions once they were reached,

the grave letters we hailed with silence

...we lived like we had no conscience.

oh Theresa, we conquered the world

but now we die depressed and alone.

we were too conceited to have known

but maybe we should have behaved.

*My heart being broken by another human being is nothing unusual
for my heart is ripped apart every sunset at the thought of a
coming tomorrow.*

<u>*Cold despair*</u>

*A tireless hopeless
sadness
like stout storm clouds
encrusts my skies,
from horizon to horizon.
footpaths to bliss
frequented in times past,
(perhaps even misused)
have all been healed,
rather - swallowed up,
claimed, by the vast
forests of needless
childish confusion.*

He had curly hair
and played the guitar.
I on the other hand
was just a gloomy guy
chasing love with words
scribbled on shabby
pieces of paper.

"Whore!" called out they
and this black eye
she smiled away,
for she ever was prey,
to the demons - poverty
coerced her not to weigh.

<u>*The monster in me*</u>

As I looked deep through the windows of her soul,
       I took in something I hadn't but should've earlier in time,
       my better half's soul gave tongue to a tale of regret and
       betrayal.

down her cheeks tears of hurt slowly rolled,
       her beautiful body polar in the radiation,
       and her breathing heavy and loud.

like leaves of an aspen in the breeze her frame was
       -indignant, she turned away slowly from my being,
       for like a midget I had kept on falling short on my pledged
       promises.

apparently, her love for me I had misplaced,
       and a loathing so deep had sprung from the loins of her
       heart,
       for this time around, I could not conjure up an excuse to
       justify why my hand had been lifted.

<u>*Cigarette smoke*</u>

It comes, as leaves to a tree
the way my mind associates,
the set transactions of life
with hopelessness and tears.
the same way, it will yoke-
affection within the sheets
and the savor of smoke
from a spree of cigarettes.

<u>*Of the dark ages*</u>

*Our duds ever black
our psyches loom dark
our fate seems bleak
but our intentions,
sculptured by light
and glazed by right
are anything but trite.*

<u>Dear Brethren</u>

I am so sorry for all the bad things I've done,
the foul language I heave against our blood,
the banes I sketch in the notebook of my mind,
when it's only you, His Shadow and I,
inside and outside Our Father's house of rite.

I wish to make known the fact that I really try,
not to throw shade on your virtuous names,
or misuse this physical frame I never deserved.
but in this mortal state I feel so weak,
I succumb to the yen of these hormones,
and the malicious whispers in my head.

I hope you bear no malice and bid my faults to oblivion,
so we can focus on the noble deeds yet to come,
like what we used to do before I lost my seraphic gifts,
we sensibly enjoy happy terms together,
with no urge to condemn your brother to Gehenna.

The massive sullen clock strikes four.
there is a distributed mess of gore
on the miserable grey wooden floor.
there's a calling crow, a broken heart,
and three black kittens torn apart.

a tall attractive body hangs aloft
a property of a long departed male.
-my vision of the sanctuary
of a dejected soul.

<u>*Time, space and pride*</u>

My sweet love,
I know it will not be long until
you and I are back together.
you are probably out there
pondering if I'm now doing well,
and puzzled about the cause
of the profound loneliness inside,
despite the room being so dense.

my sweet love,
I pray that you will be as patient
as the clocks little hand itself,
for the three things cutting off
our lonely islands at the moment,
from the furtherance of a fine
narrative for our flocks-to-come,
are time, space and pride.

<u>*...and again we shall dance*</u>

Never ask me what
it feels like,
or to explain what went on
...because I can't.
I have lost the capacity
of knowing
what really happened or what
only transpired in my head.
all I now know
is a confusion.
one that brings back
the sad; another unwanted
friend, and again
we shall dance.

<u>*Sleeping...*</u>

Against expressing resentment
of everything around me,
I took my everyday stand.
I loosen my horn from the feud,
I liberate infliction from my lungs,
I let...
palpebrae seal.
chantings sigh in my ear,
I palm what I not often perceive,
drown my dander in their libretto,
consign the world to Oblivion,
and emerge in the crook of
Morpheus' arm.

A petal from my rose
          stolen by the wind
-and negligence
          falls lazily and hurt
to kiss the dust,
          once more, before it
shrivels up to once again
          become one with the soil.

a vestige of what was
          once my beautiful rose
stands there now petal-less
          -only the thorns thriving
wanting to topple over
          from the roots upwards,
for its only reason to live
          seems to have left it too.

<u>Uncloven palisades</u>

My son, prove the world wrong,
prove all absent fathers wrong,
bid the world to cry the day you fall;
make the mountains move
and make the palisades cleave.

the day when the final bells toll,
you ought to have left a mark,
on the souls in this fading park;
make the mountains move
and make the palisades cleave.

the future must revere your name,
bid it to sing songs about you,
pen poems about lives near you.
let the theaters scream how you
made the mountains move
and made the palisades cleave.

do not just depart from this vital,
leave, like you were never here,
and your echo no good to gundy.
to leave, the mountains unsullied
and the palisades uncloven.

Dear universe I infer, reasonably
me being a virus in your system,
but if she's going to be like me
in every way within the bounds
of this unsweetened existence
then you do not fetter us,
please don't
--get me past the greeting stage.
rob me of my hearing and foul
my discernment but I beg of you
not to pluck out my eyes so I may
simply assume she's just another
pretty face like the rest of them.

<u>*Atop the hill*</u>

Cold feet in the sand, the bottle in my hand,

filled to brim with death, the perduring breath,

from this hateful earth.

the light cool breeze, percusses on my face,

but no emotions allay, my body's still to defray,

for my grief's wild buffet.

the air atop the hill, reeking of calm and thrill,

creaking of flatter and shame, fiercely all the same,

I still feel like a slave.

as the light wearies down, I gaze upon the horizon,

I petition, if I down this, my work will they miss,

and my child will they kiss?

Last week you were happy and so you noticed the gravity in her eyes. you thought cool of the black boots she wore so you walked up to her, smiling and said " hello." you came to me and admitted it was lovely. this, neither one of us can take away. now chances are the next time you will see her, you will be unsure of everything; a cynic to past personal narratives. you will beat your brains out about whether you are a subject of reality or just another object…back to your unstable fashion, a child of contradicting notions. you will tell yourself that you will not let another person's beauty be a problem of yours, that such trivialities were things that were meant to be overcome and then you will swear on a dead philosophers grave that you'll never utter a word to her again. It has happened on multiple occasions, so try not to leave a trail of confusion in the poor child's mind, doubting herself and perhaps destroying what others can actually love. Stay away.

<u>Unwinged devil</u>

*At ease with her usual standard
of unprecedented brilliance,
she who brought this gloom
upon me plants a soft kiss
on my forehead.
barring none of my will to live
she turns and walks away.
I'm left furnished with feelings,
self-debating if I should let
this fissure between us mature,
and gift the chances
of Euphrosyne ever laying her
fingers upon me to the shadows.
I may dare prophesy this body
of mine in a little while will only
be a corpse waiting
to be painted on the canvas
of some strange graveyard,
to be mixed with filth and
feasted upon by fervid worms.
perhaps I should pen a poem
with a letter for a title
or scribble for the masses
some sort of a treatise
to warn them that the winged
devils might not be the only kind.*

Hopeful refugees

Behold beloved,
brothers and sisters,
you and I
and the friend not yet
known to us,
in less than two
months time,
we shall hang our hats
in foreign land.
chances are, our sense
of being color blind,
together with our confidence,
are going to be gone.
poisonous prejudice apace
with the sun,
will wontly soar than slide,
and as if we are damned,
even the forces of nature
are bound to bestow,
a devil of a time.
as dawns die down
into days,
mother's tender loving care
we shall long for,
but from the road back home,
our itchy feet
we shall steer away.

<u>Pleasant petrichor</u>

Oh sweetest
       cumbersome rain,
muddy these
       ugly streets
with your lovely
       cleansing juices,
for with this slight
       highlight of summer,
your children.
       your children,
were starting
       to look happier,
and the girls,
       were starting
to look prettier.

<u>*In a strange hospital bed*</u>

Friendly unfamiliar faces
stare down subdued and silent
at my failing frame,
semi-supine and wrapped up
like an Egyptian mummy
in a strange hospital bed.
my feet I can't feel
my mouth I can't move
and the events which led
to this moment, I can't remember
but I feel a stinging sensation
where my skin used to be.
a sudden rush of wind
laden with the stink of kerosene
rushes up my nostrils
and there and then I remember,
I remember the iciness of the liquid
running down my forehead
and the eager sound
of a match stick catching flame,
as my demon...no, not my demon.
it was her, the love of my life,
as she lit a match to end my misery
on this wretched planet
because I'd been depressed
-for too long
and because I had almost
-cheated on her
at some party the previous evening.

<u>*A morning of nothing*</u>

Hurled by smoke
into a coughing
spree,
with my tongue
on fire
and my chest
in torment
I look at my hands
in hope
that I will find
lung particles
in my palms
...presented
with what
the universe
never fails
to endow; nothing,
in dismay...
I take another pull.

<u>*"So sorry."*</u>

Why I have not come?
I am still trying to mark,
but my center bleeds,
at the heed of things,
that come after you,
in my solid absence.

<u>*Bondage*</u>

And there had lain
a man once "The Man"
ragged and tattered,
a pond of sweat
beneath his feet
and the sun walloping
his melanin brow,
while he pined for snow.

compelled by the strap,
up on his feet he goes,
he toils and toils
upon the soil
that once was his,
but today he is-
synonymous, only to
his nabbed dignity.

Grandmother and I

She...Just a shy past eighty
lives her life elated.
today it seems in hindsight
her springtide turned out
handsome;
her friends prospering
and fiends chiefly previous,
she's still a savvy soul young
at heart.

I...a lustrum past sixteen
persist my life shaken.
with my later being hostile
when I ponder what it is
I will haul.
most friends being have
forgotten
and fiends being have
fostered,
I'm a supple soul young
at heart.

<u>*Happy birthday*</u>

Happy birthday,
to you my bosom buddy,
I know from time to time,
we might be ill at ease,
and for scores of days,
we may not touch shoulders,
but know that deep
underneath,
in the road house of my heart,
there is always a room for YOU.

<u>*In church*</u>

I cast my eyes upstairs,
In search of Numen.
I ask for kindness,
for plainly I haunt,
his house of rite,
with the false notion.

A sad,
-sad sad man,
way past his prime
lives inside of me.
a wealthy mine
of knowledge
he is, but his zest
for life is long gone
and his mind
is full of narratives
- beautiful only
in mythical memory.
his presence,
I've tried to discard
but some part of me
seems to like
his being there.

<u>A glimpse into my dotage days</u>

My days are black and blanch.
on the couch I coma alone,
from dawn to dusk, year in year out.
I enjoy no kith or kin, to come call on me,
steal my sparkle, waste my winter of life.
I sing sad songs, fry fine fishes,
and
nab numbing naps, to pass my present.
in the Garcia gardens, I take tardy walks,
and stare at sightly girls,
*   -   solely, to make them stiff.*
I am no man of means, just a puny potato,
with two tints to my life,
and I love it just the way it is.

<u>The old river and I</u>

Staring into the soul of the waters
that lay before my eyes
my old friend, once an oracle of mine
one of the many, I had forsaken
in the joy of a moment.
my discernment - dampened,
for every fragment of my mind
scurried along with bricks and stones,
in an attempt to haze the rivers gaze
into the bleak abysm of my own soul.

with a lone violent wave,
all my inner efforts are surmised useless
I'm left bare - all ego depleted
bereft of all, that could have rendered
my concealment from the scrutiny of the old river,
possible.
and thus at this moment, it struck me
I had to unfold what I had formerly tried to veil
confess how I had sensed it coming,
a seething imminence, almost palpable
-avertable,
but instead, I had opted to cast a blind eye,
I had chosen to save only myself,
from the lick of the flame,
that flickers from the inferno below.

I had meant no harm. I had had no intentions,
to hasten her final decay
- she had been only mine after all,
and I was hers, but still, I had not tried
to stop any of it.
her torrent of troubles, stemming
from needless domestic difficulties,

our Insomnia inspired tussles,
both of us almost always with a cancer stick
stuck between our index and middle fingers
and the consequential loss of our love
all because my ideas, our ideas
- our emotions getting lost in translation,
from the inner depths of our minds,
into a perplexing physical reality.

now, that her blood is on my hands,
her ghost, I'll forever let torment me
in day and in delusion but,
old friend before I take my leave,
tell me please, how could I,
a mere miserable mortal have saved her
when I too, was getting belittled
by the burden of my own existence?

<u>*Letters to L*</u>

1
Is it possible?
is it nonsensical?
not yet have we shared words,
yet I feel for millions of years,
we have paranormally
conversed.

2
Is it tart?
is it pleasant?
son of Venus please assist,
we are going to be strangers,
until one of us sees this
through!

3
Is it normal?
is it anomalous?
unstable I might be,
in a jam packed room,
it's exclusively you
and I!

4
Is it a wish?
is it a hunch?
though not yet promised,
I am going to give you love,
incomprehensible like
it's divine!

5
Is it a vision?
is it a delusion?
in the dark of the night
when you snore,
I am going to stay by your door,
to deal away with daunting
demons!

6
Is it thrill?
is it dread?
forgive my discomposure,
but I struggle in your
presence,
to keep my mind and body
together.

7
Is it sorcery?
is it science?
in the good house of rite,
your presence speaks
much louder,
than the marvellous sacred
hymns.

8
Is it Lana?
is it Leanna?
I may certainly not be sure,
but one of these
coming years,
the ropes we shall gladly
splice!

9
This is not an ode.
this is a cry for help.
for I strive with words,
but in the imminent future
I shall disembark my haze,
verge upon your pretty face,
amidst other things,
finally say hello.

<u>Goodbye</u>

Oh sweet Lana, my heart bleeds.
of the pine, I can't put in words,
but the cold hard snub I braved,
bids me to tell you nevermore,
shift your eyne in the path of my tide.

my prospects have been maimed,
by the loftiness of your being.
the bad vibes to which my soul clung,
have left my yen for you a tidy sum of smither,
which the winds of time shall blow afar.

I ponder forging missing progress,
truly, is this how our fling concludes?
the shiny morrow I had sketched,
on the canvas of my mind,
all snafued up in a heartbeat.
the tosses and turns of the night,
planning our toned posterity,
were nought but a folly!?

how I wish the puissant deity,
had shone his light upon me,
before I had cast out the line,
of my feeble bosom's rod,
deep into the comfortable flood,
of the haps presumed to betide.

now this being has given up
thrown away all the duds of hope.
fainly settled on forever being alone,
until the day the pleasing gods opt,
to free me from this blimp of sentiment.

Logos

<u>#8</u>

We faced the emptiness of existence like real bosses; we went out, we danced, we drank wine and lied. women chose us as sexual partners…we promised our bodies to many. we got in trouble and spent nights in cells. some got married and the lucky ones died. some rose up dominance hierarchies whilst others just moved around like ghosts or stayed at home, in their beds all day. these differences in difficulties meant nothing in the end. it mattered not how we had confronted the present or how we had sharpened our knives and waited to be confronted by the future, for in the end we all converged. we faced the same futility, exitus. it had been hell of a time, yes, but none of us could stand and say with their chests that it had actually been a great time.

I have never been able to define life myself despite twenty-two years of enduring it. However, I've always felt it imperative that the definition includes its character and its climax. Thus the definition I've so far felt perfect and chosen to adopt is Allan Edgar Poe's. Life, as the shadow that precedes death. Short and precise.

<u>*Perhaps*</u>

*I cringe, I cringe at the sight of them
mumbling in their multitudes like
bulimic birds,
their fair bright robes blinding my
effete eyes - but perhaps;
they have not heard.
dingy water they sprinkle like special
salve applying,
to every inch of their credulous finite
frames - perhaps again;
it's the universe entrusting me with a
fore row view,
to the unseasoned beauty of what only
Darwin discerned.*

<u>My body and mind</u>

What is this my body but an ill-fated
assemblage of decaying glands,
tobacco, alcohol and poorly prepared
meals from fast food stores?
and this mind I tend to call mine?
a shitpile of ideas internalized
from people life forced me to lend ears,
personalities I have identified with
and "facts" I was made to memorize
by the schooling system.

<u>Ignorant lives</u>

We live our lives in ignorance,
for we've accepted to settle
for far less than we deserve.
we've dehorned the heads
and defeathered the wings
of the curious beasts that live
in each and every one of us.

Humanity

This is us - humans,
spending our days
on this wretched planet;
striving, to be gods
in the eyne of man
and crafting our animality
prime
over all animate beings.

<u>Hypocrites</u>

We all down here are hypocrites,
pretending to be persons,
with a profound love for the truth,
and shamming to be persons,
with a plumbless loathing for deceit.

<u>*Haiku 1*</u>

Why should we trouble
ourselves in this semblance for
-   the presence of things?

<u>*Illusions of significance*</u>

Our existence is significant
-only in our heads,
we are ignored and neglected
by the universe,
for we are only shards in its mould.
even,
in these skull sized kingdoms
we can only truly hold the reins
-briefly,
before the wille zum leben
and its unforgiving comrades
plunge us back into despair.

Orphaned - a people they were,
by the gods their forefathers
had conjured from the depths
of their macabre minds,
solely to land sleep at night.
myriads of seasons later,
owing to gods of bypast fancies,
sleep and tears hazed their eyes,
and anything but hale at ease
they lay, wide-eyed at night.

Girl with the blue-veined breasts

Take this vinous drink, girl with the
blue-veined breasts,
I understand not why you grieve but
from the expressions
of all the voyeurs feasting on your
feminal swellings,
it surely must be something they deem
sinister.
feel no shame and indulge, there's no
right or wrong
don't be shephard by their faulty moral
compass,
shun obedience to their soi-disant
authority, after all
your sorrows don't spring from the
same source.
I too don't believe in their praised ideas
or their values,
I'm a man of unpopular ideas flirting
with slews of addictions,
plus, I'm a votary of vinous drinks too
simply trying to fill the void
by dancing straight into the arms of
death
- at least that's what they say.
but I mind not, I'll keep on being at it at a
leisurely pace,
there is no hurry in this world and
besides, it's too early
for self-abandonment into the usual
painless boredom.

<u>Like a child</u>

"Like a child who dreamt
of a monster under his bed,
in their myriads they deemed
of a higher power over their heads,
but never in the history
of modern mortals had dreams
ever conjured anything to life.
in fact belief in the unreal
had only slowly drained life
from beautiful creative minds."
-this I thought inside the walls
of the ward that stifled my friend.

<u>*#10*</u>

*I would need thousands of years of sleep to replenish the strength
the delirium of paradise in this world has wasted.*

<u>Beliefs and corpses</u>

Apace with the elfin hand
of the usual ceaseless clock,
insulting and belittling nouns,
for me the narrow-minded
believers coined and conjured,
and the raw relentless wind
of resentment, they routed
fromwards the inimitable
maker of their misfortune,
towards my forlorn frame
by virtue of their assumptions
being comparable to corpses.

<u>At the potter's</u>

As he stood in their midst,
whilst they shed their tears
over the passing
of a single insignificant soul,
one that had already survived
this senseless slavery towards nil
for more than six decades,
and bore him several siblings,
-he wondered to himself...
how could they not grasp it?
of all the horrors in the world,
why would they not celebrate
the almost blinding fact
that she had been set free
from that which maintains
itself without reason,
that she had been finally
dimmed back into oblivion?

<u>Sand in hand</u>

"This sinless smattering of cosmic soot
I will rob from its peaceful setting.
morph it into infirm animate beings
with feelings, nerves and needs.
I will crowd them with iterations
and make them worship my citations,
in a world in which woe will imbue,
until their countenances turn blue."
-thought he who they say is worthy
of the unwashed persons' alimony.

<u>Alone</u>

To have had exchanged mine
for mothers at the unfolding.
to have tarried the long days
and nights of my journey
from womb to tomb - alone,
like the last of some alien
kind, or the first.
to have never been a man
overly "odd" - as many would
like to pleasure themselves
with this thought, or anxious,
when push came to shove,
I could put on a fitting mask,
understand the to-be-dones
run with them
and be full of nonsense too.
to have not have enjoyed
the luxury of ties, friendship.
to have not loved all of them
the way they came - crooked.
to have not have found
sane reasons to be involved
in unholy couplings of puppet
and puppeteers, rather
to have had accepted peers
only as interim allies.

And I like them had been borne for months
by the torso of a woman,
with my head and knees riveted to my thorax,
it was but an omen - ill for the morn,
the morn which was set for me to witness
a nightmare laden with unavailing acts.
but I not like them, never could wield empathy
or pangs of conscience.
but this my neutrality, was it not a quality
of the gods they fitly dotted upon,
each night and day with never hints of the
daily petitioned grace?

Sun to my being

She's become, sadly...the sun to my being,
the whole sum of my existence crumpled up nicely
for another persisting human being of about
nineteen...
with futile hopes and dreams of a promised bliss
beyond the grave or at least in the later years of
life.
but then I wonder to myself, what does it matter?
aren't the very same things that lay in our ever
increasing pasts
the very same things lying for us in our receding
futures
the temporarily sufficeable necessities and
yearnings - designed simply
to keep us all at it - struggling with glimmering eyes
in this world where everything is always nothing.

It has in effect, almost become effortless for a man to find mirth in his mortal state period, for a man possesses little choice, save for to chase the soreness, to gain transitory solace.

<u>*Whispers in his ear*</u>

*By cause of those
who had been there
before him,
whispering in his ear
to slacken just
a little for it was,
not Harvard, or
anything near it,
we watched him try
to lift the curse
of the tormented genius.*

<u>#12</u>

The same thing that lies before birth, is the same thing that lies after death. It's a process infinite we have termed growth, with neither a proverbial ending nor a beginning.

<u>*#13*</u>

Only wise men will take a mortal and ponder among themselves what lies prior the egg and sperm, and only the wisest will be able to discern the actuality about existence and see that we are what we've always been, matter in metamorphosis.

<u>*Haiku 2*</u>

*An unimportant
character in a charade,
scribbled by the hordes.*

<u>Dreaming</u>

I'm sure they lied to us,
dreaming has got to be,
the greatest feeling in the world.
for;
-there's a little bit of alien guise to it,
being abducted from your zing,
where you held no reins!
-there's a little bit of insanity to it,
being allowed to play God,
sans consequences!
-there's a little bit of abuse to it,
being steered back to being,
outside your yen!

Come what may,
I impart with no sneaking suspicion,
everyone's got to be fey!
when we're cloven from the main,
the curtains drawn on our eyes,
ears hoisting pillows from below,
we still catch sight of things,
and still hearken few!

Another normal day

The smiles, the frowns.
    the heat, numb feet
     -   forty degrees feels cold.

    everything is the same
an emptiness;   all is vanity
     ...a constant.

all I thought I'd seen
    and all I believed I'd
experienced   - obscured
a fog has descended.

my reality is now almost,
always wrong and my truth
       ...slightly in accordance
with everyone else's   reality.

a hole in the ground, a cat
...Mother Theresa?
    spiders from the south,
potatoes in my mouth,
     a hundred heave in sight.

the past, the future
     little correlation;
    chance or hallucinations?
stop whispering!
I am not confused.

a common reality
     has become too complex
    because -
bears and bees are one

like bites and stings
and, I often write in Bemba.

my arms have minds
and my eyes…
stop looking at his ass
…pause.

Hope!
Hope?
Hope!?
is too risky;   optimism is a stretch
it's is a hopeless fight
sanity IS impossible.

Before the clay of a man is laid to sleep in the dust, he can only truly be defined by what he chose to struggle for in his sentience.

<u>*Am I not a god?*</u>

Am I not a god when
I have this potent pencil
and this piece of paper,
in the grip of my hands?
as I rub this prompting lead
against these maiden sheets,
I lug to life and twirl to dust
ideas in my readers heads.
objectiviness of the mind
I restore, reality I alter
and wisdom I whisper,
to the most discerning
of my trusty patrons.

If we were not being bored we were being dragged about by our physical needs, shouting and screaming, praying and playing, learning and losing but always - we found ourselves back on our feet. if it had not been for responsibility, we would have waltzed to the potter's field, a long time ago. we conversed about the same things over and over again, escaped the lesser things and fled to worse. we made the little things the bigger things. philosophizing and rationalizing everything but the answer was always right there; it was as it should have been, we were part of nature and so, all was natural. but of course if we had been born truly pure as they said, then all that happened afterwards, was the poison.

<u>*Misfit*</u>

Like a cost,
I refuse to be perfect.
like I'm lost,
I refuse to be tamed.
like a ghost,
I refuse to be forgotten.

<u>*Haiku 3*</u>

A dazed lykoi cat
escapes from it's mother's loins
-   now, nine lives poorer.

<u>*Little builders*</u>

Us, all humans
when we communicate
become little builders
going about our often tasks
trying to build our ideas
in other people's heads.

<u>#16</u>

Whether we mortals fathom the drift or not, we all are partakers in implicit verbal warfare. With every statement, somebody conquers and somebody cedes and most of the time, we clench our own two hands around our necks, decimating ourselves.

A world disunited

By cause of racial tilt,
polar preferences,
chapel convictions
and civic boarders,
we've rivalled ourselves,
like partakers of a brawl.
ditto the days of the
dinosaurs final reign,
Cosmos' long fingers,
gifting scorned liberty
from time and age,
are imminent upon us all.
if mankind truly were,
an objective species,
upon the clamped down
gates of mortality,
is where we would all
wage our war.

<u>Hope</u>

Go west go north
hope is what keeps
dreams alive.
go east go south
hope is what makes
life worthwhile.

<u>The elixir</u>

*HOPE the elixir
making our dreams
achievable
and our hardships
bearable.*

<u>The elixir</u>

*HOPE the elixir
making our dreams
achievable
and our hardships
bearable.*

they didn't want to be alone, regardless of the fact that each one of them, was a narcissistic base animal, caring only about their needs and not anyone else's (it was understandable, nature had designed them that way). thus, they deluded themselves into these conceptual worlds, these phrenic places where the favored ones were said to timely disregard the intimations of self-preservation for others. one such preposterous (and self-sustaining) place they called love. they kept it covert in the frames of their hearts - light years away from the astuteness of their intellects. most (if I may dare say – all of them) stooped down to this idea (feeling/decision/pledge) at some point. Some went mad and killed for it whilst others suicided. others got served well and promises to stay were kept. naturally, offspring sprung from their loins and they rejoiced in their recess from the abyss. the whole case was interesting, to see how an idea could easily upset the foundations of logic and turn them into dust at that very moment when anything close to paradise was anticipated. However, paradise (heaven) is only wishful.

It was a place where everything had already been figured out.
one, where only pleasantries were expected to be exchanged,
where shoulders to cry on were always readily available.
we had been told, it was a place generous to fault
the world - one big sunny place filled with endless enchantments;
content, beaming and big-hearted people.

it was, at that moment when we had started consolidating
the subjective experience of ourselves
(not just as mere extensions of those who'd brought us forth)
and the world around us,
that the instillation of these suppositions began.
us, being brave little beings with unsuspicious hope-propped eyes,
we hung on their every impression and consequently,
chorused an untroubled song.

we grew older, the song we sang got slower and solemn.
our perception of the world started to change.
we started unmasking the half-truths;
recited, sung, written, carved out and painted by the artists.
-we slowly regressed to the mean of the world.
we were getting tired of being exploited,
of being frowned upon for being different and even during this
process
we could see in the future the futility of all our actions.

when we got old, the artistry stopped altogether.
we finally gave up trying to ignore the infamies of the place.
we cast aside our pangs of conscience
and almost as if it had been what we had been born for,
it was now us, selling their souls to pay our tithes.
by conforming, to the seemly of the place
our childhood aspirations we'd misplaced because of sheer
weakness of will.

we became bitter and best friends with despair.

we then resorted to beliefs beyond rationale,
dispositions lacking warrant and principles -- antithetic to purity,
for we'd failed to understand the true reason,
why it was us who had to be involved in this puzzling cycle of
living.
we now had chosen to exist, to become seekers of perpetual
relevance,
in a passing sentience.

with the passage of time, the existential temptations;
avarice, envy, gluttony, lust, sloth, vanity and wrath we'd regaled
in them all,
but what we truly sought never came.
our failure to discover the truth about the required, the intended
and most importantly the notion of our "being,"
was clear, so we tried to unveil the secrets of our sires
but that too was in vain.
for years and years we simply waited until it was disclosed
that our desires were insatiable - and our frames had never been
designed
to carry the weight of the freedom
life had bestowed upon us.

often times, especially in the company of our loved young ones
we still try to recite, sing, write, carve and paint happy pieces
to maybe fool them into thinking that fast happy melodies are
playing
in the backgrounds of our lives,
in the hope that they will discover different paths than those,
we discovered - paths not littered by scorn and judgment
but behind these blasé aspects we are ever fraternizing
with Beethoven's saddest masterpiece
no longer tempted to exist and invariably, waiting to not being
alive.

About the Author

W.S. Prince, also known as Ryan or Friedrich's Boy was conjured in 2012. Over the years, existing mostly as an abstract concept, a pale personality and perhaps even a disorder, he became fascinated with social psychology and philosophy. These interests led to a passion for ideas and extensive reading. A Season of Decay is W.S. Prince's first book, a by-product of a larger body of work.

www.ingramcontent.com/pod-product-compliance
Lightning Source LLC
Chambersburg PA
CBHW072054150726
47999CB00005B/1774